GLADIATOR
LIFE AND DEATH IN ANCIENT ROME

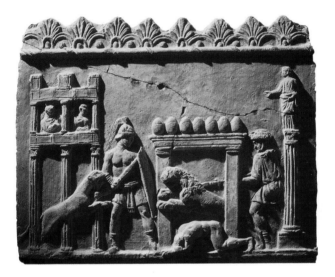

GLADIATOR
LIFE AND DEATH IN ANCIENT ROME

By
John Malam

Consultant
Guy de la Bédoyère

A DK Publishing Book

0368 8A 884

Dorling  Kindersley

LONDON, NEW YORK, MUNICH,
MELBOURNE, AND DELHI

Project Editor Steve Setford
Project Art Editor Peter Radcliffe
Senior Editor Fran Jones
Senior Art Editor Stefan Podhorodecki
Category Publisher Jayne Parsons
Managing Art Editor Jacquie Gulliver
US Editors Gary Werner and Margaret Parrish
Picture Researcher Sarah Pownall
DK Picture Library Sally Hamilton, Sarah Mills, Rose Horridge
Production Erica Rosen
DTP Designer Siu Yin Ho

First American Edition, 2002

02 03 04 05 10 9 8 7 6 5 4 3 2 1

Published in the United States by:
DK Publishing, Inc.
95 Madison Avenue
New York, NY 10016

CIP data is available from the Library of Congress.

ISBN 0–7894–8531–1 (HC)
ISBN 0–7894–8532–X (PB)

Reproduced by Colourscan, Singapore
Printed and bound by L.E.G.O., Italy

See our complete product line at **www.dk.com**

CONTENTS

INTRODUCTION

Picture the scene: a huge stadium in ancient Rome is packed with a noisy, excited crowd. They are here to watch gladiators fight to the death. Suddenly, the spectators fall silent as a fighter falls to the ground wounded. Then they start to shout in Latin *"Iugula!"* It means "Kill him!"

It's hard to imagine that anything so horrible, so bloodthirsty, could ever have happened. But to the Romans, the spectacle of highly trained fighters attacking each other with swords, daggers, lances, tridents, and nets was simply great entertainment!
   Although gladiators are long gone, the fascination with these Roman fighters is as strong as ever. Today, crowds still like to watch them perform – not in bloodstained stadiums but in movie theaters, where actors play the part of Roman fighters. As we watch the latest blockbuster film, packed with

THIS CARVING OF TWO WOMEN FIGHTING SUGGESTS THAT WOMEN MAY HAVE TAKEN PART IN GLADIATORIAL CONTESTS.

special effects, or play the latest computer game, we can imagine that we've traveled back in time to the world the Romans knew.

But what was that world really like? That's where you'll find this book helpful. You'll travel through the magnificent marble city that was ancient Rome, in Italy. You'll find out about the Romans' everyday lives, their emperors and gods, and their soldiers and empire. But most of all, you'll get to know the gladiators whose blood was spilled in the Colosseum – Rome's biggest, most awe-inspiring stadium. If there had been an Eighth Wonder of the Ancient World, this surely would have been it.

For those of you who want to explore the subject in more detail, there are "Log On" boxes that appear throughout the book. These will direct you to some fascinating websites, where you can check out even more about ancient Rome. As the Romans would have said "Mox nox in rem!" – "Let's get this show on the road!"

John Malam

DEADLY HEROES

Gladiators were the superstars of their time. They were adored by their fans and rewarded with large sums of money – just like today's music, sports, and movie stars. But there was one crucial difference between gladiators and modern crowd-pleasers – these Roman entertainers killed each other. Cold-blooded killing was their job.

LOG ON...
http://depthome.brooklyn.
cuny.edu/classics/gladiatr/

A taste for violence

Gladiators were a Roman fashion – the world has seen nothing like them before or since. In towns and cities throughout the Roman Empire, arenas of all sizes were built to stage shows for the public – especially gladiatorial games. These violent, bloody contests were usually the most popular event in a town's social calendar, a chance for people to see their heroes in action. Roman audiences were as happy to watch gladiators spilling each other's blood as they were to watch actors perform a comedy play at the theater. The Romans thought that gladiator fights were a perfectly acceptable form of entertainment. It was gory but glamorous, and they loved it. It's only later generations – and that includes us – who think of them as horrible acts of violence, the nastiest, cruelest blood sport ever invented.

B ringers of good luck

The Roman liking for watching fighting and killing in public lasted for some 500 years. It's not surprising, then, that gladiators played such a big part in Roman society. All kinds of superstitions and beliefs grew up around them. For example, during a marriage ceremony it was the custom on the wedding day for the bride to part her hair with the tip of a spear – and if it had belonged to a gladiator killed in the

THIS PICTURE CAPTURES THE DRAMA OF THE ARENA. A FALLEN GLADIATOR LOOKS TO THE CROWD TO SEE IF THEY WILL SPARE HIS LIFE. THEIR "THUMBS DOWN" RESPONSE SIGNALS THAT THE LOSER SHOULD DIE.

9

arena, she would be blessed with good luck. Perhaps the meaning of this strange act was to drive out harmful spirits believed to be tangled in her hair. Customs such as this show how fascinating gladiators were to ordinary Roman people.

Feared fighters

The truth is, underneath this fascination with gladiators lay a tremendous fear of them. It was because gladiators were professional fighters, trained in the brutal art of committing public executions, that they scared most Romans. There are records of gladiators who escaped from their training schools and went on the rampage, killing anyone who got in their way.

The Romans had a love-hate relationship with gladiators. They loved watching these

THE LAST GLADIATOR CONTESTS TOOK PLACE 1,600 YEARS AGO

powerful fighters battle it out in the arena from the safety of their ringside seats, but they hated the thought of gladiators getting out into society and running wild. You can compare gladiators with wild beasts – entertaining to watch from a safe distance, but best avoided if charging toward you!

THIS IS A TOMBSTONE OF A RETIARIUS – A GLADIATOR WHO FOUGHT WITH A NET AND A THREE-PRONGED SPEAR CALLED A TRIDENT.

Lowest of the low

Gladiators held a low position in Roman society, way down at the bottom with slaves and criminals. For example, once in a time of food shortages, the gladiators were sent out of Rome so that they wouldn't eat too much of the city's dwindling grain supply.

A slain gladiator was not usually buried in the public cemetery. This only happened if the corpse was claimed by the gladiator's master, family, or friends, who could pay for a decent funeral. The bodies of many dead gladiators were just tossed into pits along with the corpses of executed criminals and people who had committed suicide.

Despite their low position in society, gladiators were not

IN THIS SCENE FROM A MOSAIC MADE IN THE AD 300S, A VICTORIOUS GLADIATOR STANDS OVER THE BODY OF HIS VICTIM.

WEIRD WORLD
IF A ROMAN MAN HAD A DREAM INVOLVING A TYPE OF GLADIATOR KNOWN AS A *THRAX*, IT WAS TAKEN AS A SIGN THAT HE WAS GOING TO MARRY A RICH WOMAN!

short of admirers. Those who fought well and lived to see another day attracted fans, many of whom were women. We know this from the graffiti they left on the walls of arenas in which their heroes fought. At the arena in Pompeii, a small Roman town in southern Italy, a gladiator named Celadus was described as a "girls' hero" and a

11

THIS BRONZE HELMET PROTECTED THE GLADIATOR'S HEAD, THROAT, AND NECK.

"heartthrob,"
while another, called Crescens,
was hailed as "the boss."

The emperor-gladiator

You'd be shocked if you saw
your country's leader fighting
in public – unless, that is, you
were at a gladiatorial contest
in Rome in the AD 180s and
190s. If you'd gone to the
Colosseum, which was the
place to see the heroes of the
arena, you might have seen the
Emperor Commodus fighting
as a gladiator. Think about it –
the leader of Rome fighting for
his life! Gladiators were admired
for their bravery. Their daring
deeds gripped the public's
imagination, and Commodus
wanted to be admired in the
same way. Although he wanted
to fight like a gladiator, he

GLADIATORS FOUGHT ONE-TO-ONE, AS
SHOWN IN THIS MODERN REENACTMENT.

had in Roman society – all the way to the top. But how did Rome's terrifying terminators come about? Well, the story of gladiators goes hand in hand with Rome's development from a cluster of tiny villages into the greatest power of the ancient world.

didn't want to die like one. He boasted that he had beaten 12,000 opponents, fighting some 735 times without getting hurt. Ordinary gladiators were lucky if they made it into double figures before biting the dust.

Unfair fights

The secret of Commodus's success was that he was a highly accomplished fighter. But sometimes he fixed the fights. Once, all the men in Rome who had lost their feet from disease or accidents were forced to fight him! They only had sponges to throw instead of stones, and Commodus killed them with a club. He also executed wild animals. During one 14-day bloodbath, he slaughtered 100 bears from the safety of the arena.

Commodus, the emperor-gladiator, is just one example of how much influence gladiators

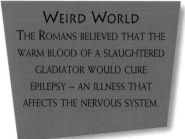

EMPEROR COMMODUS FRIGHTENED PEOPLE WITH HIS DERANGED BEHAVIOR. IN THE END, HIS COURTIERS HAD HIM ASSASSINATED WHILE HE WAS IN HIS BATH.

THE RISE OF ROME

By AD 300, Rome was the grandest city on Earth and the center of a massive empire. Home to about 1.5 million people, it was a fabulous place, with sumptuous palaces, grand statues, magnificent triumphal arches celebrating Rome's victories, and, of course, the Colosseum – the finest gladiator stadium in the Roman Empire. Often, the Roman people wondered how and when it had all begun.

The wolf and the twins

Like many peoples of the ancient world, the Romans made up stories to explain things about themselves and their world. In time, these stories, or myths, became accepted as true facts rather than invented tales.

To explain the origins of their city, the Romans told one of the best-known myths of all time – the story of the twin boys Romulus and Remus. In the story, the two boys were thrown into the Tiber River on the instructions of their great-uncle, King Amulius. The king wanted them to die so they would never find out about the cruel things he had done to their family. Amulius was afraid that if they lived they would take revenge on him.

But Romulus and Remus did not die. They were discovered by a she-wolf who fed them with her own milk until a shepherd took them home and brought them up as his own sons. They grew into strong young men, and when they learned about Amulius they

WEIRD WORLD
MARCUS AGRIPPA (63–12 BC) IMPROVED ROME'S WATERWORKS. IN 33 BC, THE CITY'S GREATEST SEWER WAS CLEANED. AGRIPPA SAILED THROUGH IT IN A BOAT TO INSPECT THE WORK!

went to his city and killed him – just as he had feared.

Having avenged their family, the brothers decided to build a city of their own, on the banks of the Tiber River. But, like all brothers, they argued – they

ROME WAS AT ITS FINEST IN THE AD 300S. AT THE CITY'S HEART WAS THE COLOSSEUM, THE OVAL BUILDING SHOWN IN THIS MODEL.

MADE IN ABOUT 500 BC, THIS BRONZE STATUE OF A SHE-WOLF SUCKLING BABY BOYS REMINDED ROMANS OF THE LEGENDARY BEGINNINGS OF THEIR GREAT CITY.

couldn't decide which of them should be the king or what the city should be called. They fought, and in the struggle Romulus killed Remus. It was left to Romulus to build the city alone, which he named Rome, after himself.

Ancient Roman historians managed to figure out a date for the founding of Rome. They said that their city was founded in the year 753 BC. This date, as it turns out, isn't far off the date used by modern historians.

The truth about Rome

The real story of Rome, as discovered by archaeologists, begins 3,000 years ago, some time around 1000 BC. This was when settlers arrived in a region that ran along the west coast of central Italy. The settlers were farmers, and they recognized that the region's fertile soil would be good for growing their crops and for raising farm animals. They built their villages on the summits of a group of seven low-lying hills, near a crossing over the Tiber River, the region's largest

THIS COIN DEPICTS ROMA, THE PATRON GODDESS OF ROME. CITIZENS OF ROME WORSHIPPED HER AND ASKED HER TO PROTECT THEIR CITY.

river. The villages prospered and grew in size. Within less than 300 years they had spread out across the hilltops, and by about 750 BC they had joined together to form a town. It was this early town that marked the birth of the city that would later become known as Rome.

The hated kings of Rome

Rome lay in a region called Latium. It was one of many rival city-states (you can think of them as "tribal areas") into which Italy was divided. The inhabitants of the city-state of Latium were known as Latins. Immediately to their north was the region of Etruria, the home of a cultured people called the Etruscans. For a time, Etruria was the most powerful city-state in central Italy, and ruled its neighbor, Latium. The Etruscans gained control of the city, and for about 100 years the city was controlled by Etruscan kings.

By 509 BC, the Latin people had had enough of Etruscan rule. They rebelled and threw Tarquin the Proud, the last of the hated Etruscan kings, out of Rome. From then on, Rome was ruled by a group of its leading citizens. It had become a

LOG ON...
www.historyforkids.org/
learn/romans/ is fact-packed!

A FARMER FROM ROMAN TIMES WOULD STILL RECOGNIZE TODAY'S COUNTRYSIDE NEAR ROME, WITH ITS OLIVE AND CYPRESS TREES, VINEYARDS, AND SMALL FIELDS.

republic – a state or country governed by politicians elected by the people.

From republic to empire

The Roman Republic lasted for almost 500 years, from 509 BC to 27 BC. During this long time, Rome was ruled by the Senate – a group of men who came from leading Roman families. The senators, as they were known, pledged that Rome would never again be in the hands of just one powerful person, such as a king.

Day-to-day decision-making was left in the hands of officials known as magistrates, who were elected for one year at a time. The two most important magistrates were the consuls. These men had the power to pass laws and declare war on Rome's enemies. Each consul checked the work of the other, to make sure that neither became too powerful.

THE SHADED AREAS ON THIS MAP SHOW THE GROWTH OF ROMAN TERRITORY.

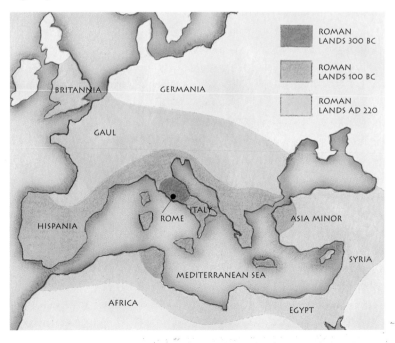

ROMAN LANDS 300 BC

ROMAN LANDS 100 BC

ROMAN LANDS AD 220

BRITANNIA

GERMANIA

GAUL

HISPANIA

ROME

ITALY

ASIA MINOR

SYRIA

MEDITERRANEAN SEA

AFRICA

EGYPT

The rise of Rome

It was during the years of the Roman Republic that Rome developed into the strongest Rome's two most brilliant generals, Pompey the Great (106–48 BC) and Julius Caesar (100–44 BC). Against all the

BY AD 120, AS MANY AS 50 MILLION PEOPLE LIVED UNDER ROMAN RULE

force in Italy. Rome gradually overpowered Italy's other city-states and brought them under its control. A long series of wars fought against Carthage, a major power based in North Africa, ended in victory for Rome in 146 BC. This triumph left Rome as the greatest power in the Mediterranean. Over the following 100 years Rome – backed by the might of its army – took control of vast tracts of land, from Spain and France in the west to Greece and Syria in the east.

Civil war!

Rome's rise to power would not have been possible without strong armies led by powerful generals. During the closing years of the Roman Republic, a civil war broke out between

DURING THE ROMAN REPUBLIC, POWER LAY IN THE HANDS OF THE SENATORS. EVERY YEAR, THE PEOPLE VOTED TO ELECT CERTAIN SENATORS TO BE GOVERNMENT OFFICIALS.

19

odds, Caesar defeated Pompey. Julius Caesar made himself the the dictator of Rome – a single ruler with more power than the

have again. A plot was hatched, and Caesar was murdered, stabbed to death in the Senate house in 44 BC.

CAESAR WORE A CROWN OF LAUREL LEAVES TO HIDE HIS BALD PATCH!

magistrates. To the proud Romans, Caesar had become too much like a king – the type of leader they never wanted to

The first emperor

Caesar's death solved nothing. Civil war flared up again as other generals fought to take control. Among them was Octavian (63 BC–AD 14), the nephew of Julius Caesar.

In 31 BC, Octavian defeated his enemies. He was now the sole ruler of Rome. But Octavian knew that the Senate and the Roman people would never accept this. So, in 27 BC, he offered to hand his powers back to the Senate, saying it was his way of bringing peace to the Roman world.

It was a clever move and the turning point in Rome's history. The Senate accepted Octavian's offer, but still left him with immense power. He was given a new name, Augustus, which meant

POMPEY (LEFT) HOPED TO BECOME THE ROMAN LEADER, BUT HE WAS MURDERED. HIS HEAD WAS OFFERED TO HIS RIVAL, JULIUS CAESAR, WITH THE WORDS "DEAD MEN DO NOT BITE"!

JULIUS CAESAR IS MURDERED. WHILE POPULAR WITH ORDINARY PEOPLE, CAESAR HAD MANY POLITICAL ENEMIES.

the "revered one." He had become the first emperor. The Roman Empire had begun! For the next 500 years, Rome was ruled by emperors.

Rome, city of marble

Augustus once said of Rome, "I inherited it brick and left it marble." He meant that he had rebuilt the city and given it fine buildings made from the best-quality stone. He wasn't alone. Many of the emperors who came after him stamped their own identities on the city, erecting ever grander buildings and monuments.

At the heart of Rome was the Forum – a narrow rectangular space that became the political, commercial, religious, and social center of the entire Roman world. The Forum was surrounded by government buildings, law courts, and temples. Politicians gave speeches from platforms in the Forum, listened to by crowds of Roman citizens. Victory parades marched through the Forum, and criminals were

UNDER THE NEW NAME AUGUSTUS, OCTAVIAN BECAME THE FIRST ROMAN EMPEROR. HE DECLARED PEACE THROUGHOUT THE ROMAN WORLD.

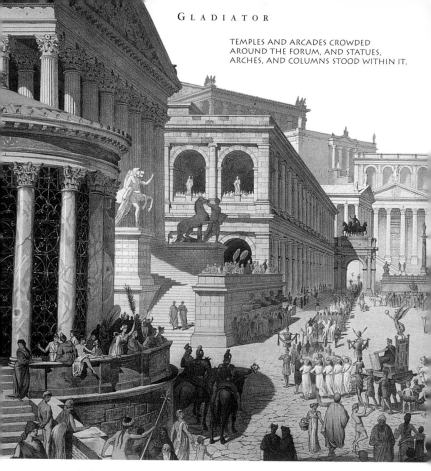

TEMPLES AND ARCADES CROWDED AROUND THE FORUM, AND STATUES, ARCHES, AND COLUMNS STOOD WITHIN IT.

executed there. It was even home to gladiatorial contests and wild beast shows, until Emperor Vespasian constructed a new showground nearby. He built a vast oval-shaped arena which was known as the Flavian Amphitheater, after his family name. It eventually acquired a new name…the Colosseum.

Bigger and better

Rome continued to grow, and in the AD 300s a list was made of all its buildings. Here's part of what the surveyors recorded. There were 28 libraries, 8 bridges, 11 town squares (*fora*), 10 basilicas, 19 aqueducts delivering 170 million gallons (760 million liters) of water a day, 1,352 drinking fountains, 11 big bath-houses and 856 small ones, 3 theaters, 29 main roads, 2 racetracks (circuses), 2 amphitheaters, 36 triumphal arches, 37 gates in the city wall (which was 31 miles [50 km]

and were amazed by what they saw. To guide them, a "street map," known as the *Forma Urbis*, was put up in a prominent place. Measuring an enormous 60 by 45 ft (18 by 14 m), it was carved onto rectangular marble slabs in the early AD 200s. Every street, building, room, and staircase in Rome was shown on it.

Unfortunately for us, this unique map got smashed to pieces long ago. Archaeologists have so far found 1,163 pieces of it. But this amounts to a mere 15 percent of the total, so 85 percent of the map is still missing. The hunt is on to find the rest of this giant jigsaw!

long), 290 warehouses, 254 cornmills, 1,797 houses owned by wealthy citizens, 46,602 apartments and small houses, and, bottom of the list, 144 public lavatories!

THE COLOSSEUM GOT ITS NAME FROM A GIGANTIC STATUE, OR COLOSSEUS, OF THE EMPEROR NERO THAT STOOD CLOSE BY.

Map of stone

Just like today's great cities, tourists visited Rome

LEGIONNAIRES AND LEADERS

Rome was one of the world's first superpowers, led by skillful men who were politicians, generals, and emperors. These ambitious leaders were determined to make Rome, and themselves, great. Some succeeded, but others were tyrants who fell out of favor with the people, and with Rome's greatest asset — the army.

Rome's all-conquering army
The Roman army was a truly formidable fighting machine, and its generals were skilled in the crafts of warfare — from hand-to-hand combat to long sieges. They were determined to win at any cost. After one of Julius Caesar's famous battles he said, *"Veni, vidi, vici,"* ("I came, I saw, I conquered"). These words became a battle cry for the army as Rome's brave

THE TACTICS AND EQUIPMENT OF IMPERIAL ROMAN SOLDIERS ARE RECREATED HERE BY DEDICATED MODERN ENTHUSIASTS.

soldiers won victory after victory, defeating enemies and taking control of their lands.

Roman soldiers were highly trained and well-equipped. Those who had the misfortune to face them in battle were lucky if they survived to fight

Organizing the army

Good organization was the key to the army's success. At first, the whole of the Roman army was known as the *legio*, a Latin word for levy, which means "to raise an army." But during the 300s BC, the army was split into

THE LARGEST CATAPULTS COULD HURL ROCKS 1,600 FT (500 M)

another day – unless, that is, they were taken prisoner. If this happened, they were likely to end up as one of the next generation of gladiators, many of whom were prisoners of war.

divisions called legions, each containing a large number of legionnaires (infantrymen or foot soldiers). There was also a small cavalry force, but it wasn't as important as the infantry.

25

ROMAN ARMOR CHANGED OVER THE
CENTURIES. THIS IS A REPLICA OF ARMOR
WORN BY LEGIONNAIRES IN THE AD 100S.

R eforming general

In the 100s BC, Gaius Marius
(157–86 BC), a leading politician
and general, introduced some
major reforms to the military.
One was to make the troops
full-time soldiers, rather than
part-timers. Another was to let
poor men join the army. Also,
soldiers were to be
paid and
equipped by
the state
for the
first time.
The changes
brought about
by Marius helped
the Roman army
become the supreme
fighting force of its time.

A natomy of a legion

From about AD 70, a legion
consisted of 5,500 men. It
was divided into 10 cohorts,
plus cavalry and officers.
The first cohort contained
the legion's 800 finest
soldiers – its crack troops.
The other nine cohorts
each had 480 men.
Within the cohorts,
soldiers were split
into groups called
centuries, each of
which had 80 men

SOLDIERS MARCHED 20 MILES (30 KM) A DAY. BOOTS WITH HARD-WEARING IRON STUDS ON THE SOLES WERE ESSENTIAL.

Weapons and armor

During the AD 100s, when the army reached its greatest strength, with some 300,000 men, legionnaires were issued with fairly standard gear. Weapons included a dagger (*pugio*), a short sword (*gladius*), and a heavy javelin (*pilum*) whose point would snap off or bend on impact, making it impossible to be thrown back by the enemy.

Legionnaires wore strips of

(at one time it was 100 men).

Centuries were themselves broken down into the smallest units of all – squads of eight soldiers who would share a tent together while they were on campaign. Each century was led by a centurion. Above him were six officers, called tribunes, who advised the legion's commanding officer, the legate.

THE SHORT SWORD WAS THE LEGIONNAIRE'S MAIN WEAPON FOR CLOSE-RANGE FIGHTING. THIS ONE IS IN ITS SCABBARD. THE JAVELIN WAS THROWN FROM A DISTANCE.

WEIRD WORLD

ON THE MARCH, LEGIONNAIRES CARRIED UP TO 90 LB (40 KG) OF EQUIPMENT ON THEIR BACKS. THEY WERE NICKNAMED "MARIUS'S MULES," AFTER THE GENERAL WHO HAD IMPROVED THE ROMAN ARMY.

flexible metal and leather armor on their bodies. Metal helmets protected their heads, cheeks, and necks. Their large, rectangular shields deflected enemy missiles, and they could also be overlapped to form all-around protection for a group of men. On the march, the legionnaire carried not only his weapons and armor, but also a weighty set of digging tools, which he needed when the legion stopped to make camp.

Conditions of service

Life was tough for a legionnaire. Some complained of harsh treatment. For those sent to the farthest outposts of the Roman Empire, the weather was an added problem. For example, one soldier stationed in northern Britain asked for woolen socks, underpants, and sandals – presumably he found the cool, wet climate very different from the one in his homeland, wherever that was.

Legionnaires joined the army for between 20 and 25 years. They were not officially allowed to marry, but many did. They learned new skills and usually received regular pay, as well as good medical treatment. On leaving the army they were given land, although this was eventually changed to a gift of

HADRIAN'S WALL IN NORTHERN BRITAIN WAS A FRONTIER OF THE ROMAN EMPIRE. BEYOND IT LIVED NONROMAN PEOPLE. THE ROMANS CALLED THEM BARBARIANS.

WEIRD WORLD
THE WORST PUNISHMENT FACED BY A COHORT WAS THE PRACTICE OF DECIMATION, WHEN THE SOLDIERS LINED UP AND EVERY TENTH MAN WAS CLUBBED OR STONED TO DEATH. ("DECI" MEANS TEN, AS IN THE WORD DECIMAL.)

money equal to 12 years' pay. After completing their military service, men were free to return to their homes, but many chose to stay in the countries where they had been posted.

Citizens and noncitizens

All legionnaires were Roman citizens – men who had rights that others did not (such as being able to vote in elections). However, not all soldiers were legionnaires. Many were non-citizens who came from the 40 or so provinces (territories) of the Roman Empire. Known as auxiliaries, these provincial troops played a vital role in defending the borders of the empire and the millions of people who lived within it. At the end of his service, an auxiliary soldier was granted Roman citizenship, which improved his status in society.

The emperor's bodyguards

Augustus, the first Roman emperor, created a special group of soldiers known

LOG ON...
www.esg.ndirect.co.uk/ for Roman army reenactments

ON PARADE, THE PRAETORIAN GUARD WORE DECORATED ARMOR. AT OTHER TIMES THEY WORE PLAIN ARMOR.

as the Praetorian Guard. It was a force of up to 10,000 carefully chosen men, whose duty was to protect the emperor from injury and rebellions. The Praetorians lived in their own barracks on the outskirts of Rome. Emperors after Augustus continued to use the Praetorians as their personal bodyguards, but as time passed the political power of these elite soldiers grew. If they disliked an emperor, they might murder him and replace him with a leader they preferred.

A risky job

It was customary for Roman soldiers to cheer a victorious general, calling out *"Imperator!,"* meaning "our commander" or "our emperor." An ambitious general might take this as a sign that the army wanted him to be emperor. If he felt he had enough support, both from the troops and from the Senate, he could make a bid to take over when the old leader died. For

because it was cheaper to do this than to buy meat from the market! However, a handful, including Trajan, were great leaders, loved by their people and dreaded by their enemies.

THE PRAETORIANS MURDERED AT LEAST 15 ROMAN EMPERORS

this reason, an emperor could never afford to fall out with the army, and there was always a chance that one of the generals was plotting to overthrow him.

Emperors good and bad
About 175 men claimed the title of emperor during the 500 years of the Roman Empire. Some had no rights to it at all, such as Postumus, who seized power while Gallienus, the rightful emperor, was away from Rome. Others, like Marius (not the general who reformed the army), held the title only briefly. One Roman writer said that Marius was emperor for just two days!

Some emperors were tyrants, feared for their cruelty. Caligula, for example, fed prisoners to the wild beasts kept at the arena,

It was during Trajan's reign that the Roman Empire reached its greatest extent, and many new buildings were put up in Rome.

ON TRAJAN'S COLUMN IN ROME THERE IS A DECORATION THAT SHOWS SCENES FROM THE EMPEROR'S BATTLE VICTORIES.

CRUEL COLOSSEUM

R ome's mighty Colosseum opened to the public in the year AD 80. To celebrate the event, 100 days of gory games were held there. Scores of gladiators were killed and up to 5,000 animals a day were butchered. This was only the start. For the next 400 bloodstained years, the Colosseum was to be the Roman world's premier killing ground.

A n awe-inspiring arena

No one knows who designed the Colosseum, but one thing's certain – it was built to last. It took about 10 years to put up the massive oval-shaped arena, which was fast work in those days. The finished building stood some 164 ft (50 m) high and measured 616 by 512 ft (188 by 156 m). Hard-wearing materials were used. The foundations and upper levels were formed from concrete, the outer wall used travertine

CORRIDOR

SEATING

(a whitish limestone), and the tiers of seating were made from white marble, which was transported by ship along the Tiber River. Blocks of stone were moved by treadmill cranes.

These were operated by workers who walked, like hamsters, inside huge wheels. As the wheels turned they pulled on ropes that raised and lowered the building stones into place.

Seats, safety, and sun

The Colosseum could seat about 45,000 people, with room for an additonal 5,000 standing.

People were seated according to their status in Roman society – the more important you were, the nearer the killing you sat. Of course, the emperor had the best seat in the building, right at the front of one of the arena's long sides. His family, friends, and favorites sat nearby. Women had the worst seats, right at the top of the

SPECTATORS REACHED THEIR SEATS VIA CORRIDORS AND STAIRCASES.

ANIMAL FIGHTS WERE POPULAR. HERE, A BEAR MAULS A BEAST-FIGHTER, WHILE TWO MEN USE WHIPS TO BEAT IT AWAY.

The building was designed so that it could be emptied quickly and safely at the end of a show, with crowds spewing from its *vomitoria* (openings) onto the city streets. There were 80 of these entrance-and-exit places, of which the public could use 76. Two were for the emperor and his courtiers, and two were for gladiatorial processions.

On hot days a canopy was stretched across the arena to give shade for the spectators, so they could watch the suffering in the arena in comfort! This

building. Seated below them were slaves and the poor, then soldiers and ordinary citizens, civil servants and officers, and finally, closest to the ringside, senators and their guests.

With so many spectators crammed inside, crowd control in the Colosseum was essential.

THE FLOOR OF THE COLOSSEUM IS LONG GONE, SO TODAY'S VISITORS CAN SEE THE UNDERGROUND PASSAGES AND CHAMBERS.

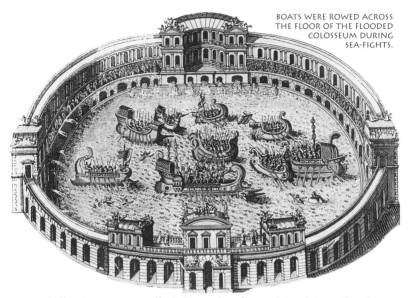

BOATS WERE ROWED ACROSS THE FLOOR OF THE FLOODED COLOSSEUM DURING SEA-FIGHTS.

vast, billowing cover, called the *velarium*, was operated by sailors. They were used to working with ships' ropes and canvas sails – the same materials that the *velarium* was made from.

that floated on this artificial lake. When these naval battles went out of fashion, a network of passages was built beneath the arena floor. In this gloomy underworld, animals were kept

THE ENTIRE COLOSSEUM COULD BE EVACUATED IN THREE MINUTES

Sea-fights in the city

When the Colosseum was first built, it was possible to flood the floor of the arena, because the ground beneath was solid and water did not leak away. If you'd been in the crowd at one of the early games, you might have seen a sea-fight, when gladiators fought on the decks of ships

in pens, ready to be sent up to their slaughter. Other parts of this hot, noisy labyrinth housed gladiators – the stars of the show who were about to have their moment of glory or disaster. For beasts and gladiators alike, there was no turning back. It was time to entertain the excited crowd, who were baying for blood!

35

MADE TO FIGHT

Gladiators were made, not born. Only the most unfortunate people became gladiators. They were sent to schools where they were given lessons in stabbing, slashing, and strangling. Pupils were taught a simple rule – do it to him before he does it to you!

IN ORDER TO BECOME A HERO OF THE ARENA, A GLADIATOR FIRST HAD TO LEARN THE ART OF KILLING.

Six gladiators and a funeral
In 264 BC, there was a fight at a Roman funeral. It was the funeral of one of Rome's wealthy citizens, Decimus Junius Brutus Pera. The six men who fought in his honor were probably the first gladiators to perform in Rome. These fighters weren't performing just to entertain the living – they were also there to give thanks for the dead man's life. It was a way of keeping his

A TOMB CARVING OF GLADIATORS FROM ABOUT 30 BC. IT MAY BE A SCENE FROM A DEAD MAN'S FUNERAL GAMES.

memory alive in the minds of the living, so that he wouldn't be forgotten.

At this time, some 350 years before the Colosseum was built, there were no arenas to fight in. Instead, the men who performed at this small show fought in the city's cattle market. No one who witnessed their contest could possibly have guessed that it marked the start of Rome's liking for blood sports.

S pilling the blood

The idea of a fight at a funeral seems strange to our way of thinking. But it wasn't like this for the Romans. The Etruscans before them may have staged fights at funerals, in which a person was sacrificed. Perhaps the Romans liked the idea so much that they copied it. The sole purpose of gladiatorial games at funerals was to spill blood – it was a "gift" from the living to the dead. In their wills, wealthy or important Romans often asked for funeral games (*munera*) to be held in their honor. In staging the games, families paid respect to their dead relatives. Because funeral games were expensive, few families could afford them, so

WEIRD WORLD
TO INSPIRE THEIR "STUDENTS," GLADIATOR TRAINERS TOLD STORIES OF BRAVE MEN WHO HAD FOUGHT WELL, SURVIVED, AND ENDED UP OWNING GRAND HOUSES, SLAVES, AND EVEN THEIR OWN GLADIATORS.

they became a way for the rich to show off their wealth in public.

Funeral games gradually grew in popularity in Rome. Records tell us that in 216 BC, 22 pairs of gladiators fought at a funeral; and at a funeral in 183 BC there were 60 pairs of fighters. As the games grew in size and became more exciting to watch, larger crowds turned up.

For many years, gladiatorial contests were held in the Forum, the city's main square. With the opening of the Colosseum, in AD 80, the crowds flocked to this custom-built killing ground. By then, gladiators were part of Roman life. The shows became bigger, bloodier, and more spectacular than ever.

Victims and volunteers

Gladiators were a commodity to be bought and sold, just like cattle. The last thing anyone

A GLADIATOR HAD ABOUT THREE FIGHTS A YEAR – IF HE SURVIVED!

wanted was a shortage of gladiators. Fortunately, there was a constant supply of victims. Most of the gladiators were outcasts from society – prisoners of war, criminals, or slaves. These were men from the lowest level of society, who had no choice about their fate.

Can you believe that some Roman citizens volunteered to become gladiators? Men with no work to do or who had lost

THE RUINS OF ROME'S FORUM, WHERE GLADIATORS ONCE FOUGHT. WOODEN SEATING WAS PUT UP FOR THE SPECTATORS.

their fortunes actually chose to become gladiators. They knew that they would be fed three times a day, have a place to sleep, receive money for every fight, and be given medical care for their injuries. But most of all, they knew that if they could survive long enough they would be free to return to their families – hopefully with enough money to start their lives over again. This much was good news.

The bad news was that volunteers had to swear an oath. They had to agree to be branded, shackled with chains, whipped with rods, pay for their food with their blood, and, if the worst

VERCINGETORIX, LEADER OF THE GAULS, SURRENDERS TO JULIUS CAESAR IN 52 BC. THE ROMANS FORCED MANY PRISONERS OF WAR TO BECOME GLADIATORS.

happened, to be killed.

If you think it was only men who fought in the arena, think again. Emperor Domitian put on shows involving women. But a later emperor, Septimius Severus, banned any fights between women in AD 200. He disapproved of women

THIS CARVING SHOWS TWO WOMEN GLADIATORS FIGHTING WITH DAGGERS. THEIR NAMES, AMAZON AND ACHILLIA, MAY HAVE BEEN STAGE NAMES.

THE GLADIATOR SCHOOL IN POMPEII, WHERE MEN WERE TRAINED TO FIGHT BEFORE APPEARING IN THE TOWN'S ARENA.

working as gladiators. The rest of Roman society, however, enjoyed their deadly duels.

Schools for gladiators

Businessmen called *lanistae,* meaning "butchers," found a way of making money out of gladiators. They worked as managers for groups of fighters, hiring them out for fights in return for money. Some *lanistae* became very wealthy doing this.

Gladiators were taught the craft of killing at special schools called *ludi.* They were large, well-run places, like army camps. The men lived in barracks and were only allowed out of the school when they had to appear in a contest. Discipline was strict, and men who broke the rules were punished by being sent to the school's prison.

Sick or injured men were no use to anyone, so trainee gladiators were well taken care of. They were given plenty of boiled beans and stodgy barley to eat – foods that filled them up and made their muscles strong (gladiators were nicknamed *hordearii,* meaning "barley men"). Their health was just as important as their

bulging muscles. Injuries and
Illnesses were treated by the
school's highly skilled doctors.

Teachers and techniques

Trainees were taught by older
men who were once gladiators
themselves. They had retired
from the arena and gone on to
work as teachers. All schools
had a small arena where teachers
taught their pupils how to fight.
At first, new gladiators practiced
fighting against a tall wooden
post, called a *palus*, which was
rammed into the ground. The
men were told to imagine the
post was their enemy, and they
attacked it with weapons chosen
by their teacher. Sometimes
they fought against a "man
of straw" – a soft, squishy,
body-shaped sack.
Like the wooden
post, it couldn't
fight back.

IN THIS MOVIE SCENE, A
TRAINER MARKS OUT
TARGET ZONES ON THE
BODY OF SPARTACUS,
SO OPPONENTS
WILL KNOW
WHERE
TO AIM.

Men learned how to fight
by using wooden swords and
other blunt weapons. It was
too risky to let them use real
weapons until they could be
trusted with them – just in c
they used them against their
teachers and escaped from t
school, or tried to commit
suicide. Only after lots of
training were they allowed
practice against other gladi

The men who trained an
lived together at a gladiato
school got to know each o
very well, and they proba
became friends. They wer
known as a *familia gladiato*
("family of gladiators").
fights they had v
pretend, and r
really got hu
However, w
it was time
entertain t
crowd and
for real, t
knew th
end up
their fr

INTO THE ARENA

You are a trained gladiator at the peak of physical fitness. The day of the games is almost here, and you are soon to enter the arena. But how will you fight? Who will you fight, and what weapons will you use? Will you live to see another day? We can only guess what went through the minds of Rome's brave gladiators as they prepared for their few minutes of fame.

THIS STATUETTE SHOWS A THRAX GLADIATOR WEARING LEG PROTECTORS, A CRESTED HELMET, AND AN ARM GUARD.

The show comes to town
Gladiatorial shows were megaexpensive, and only the wealthiest citizens – and emperors – could afford to put them on. Shows were advertised days before a troupe of gladiators reached town. Painted signs appeared on the walls and excitement grew among the public. Town criers walked the streets calling out the fighters' names and skills, while other men carried banners broadcasting the same news. Get-rich-quick merchants set up souvenir stalls close to the arena, selling gladiator goodies – from pottery models of gladiators to decorated oil lamps. This buildup ensured that every show was sold out before the big day.

SOME GLADIATORS REFUSED TO EAT BEFORE THE GAMES – NOT EVEN DISHES LIKE THIS ASPARAGUS AND QUAIL – IN CASE THEY WERE TOO FULL TO FIGHT.

One last supper

Gladiators came to town the day before the games began. They were guests of the wealthy man (known as the *editor*) who was giving the show. That night he gave a grand banquet in their honor, and the public watched them eat. It was a chance to "eye up" the gladiators and decide who looked like they'd fight well, and who wouldn't. The men knew that this might be the last food they'd ever eat. Some made the most of it and stuffed their faces – can you blame them? A few men couldn't stomach the food and spent the evening pleading with members of the public to take messages to their families.

GAMES BEGAN WITH ANIMAL FIGHTS. THIS FIGHTER FACES A LION AND A LEOPARD.

A REFEREE ENSURES THAT TWO GLADIATORS KEEP TO THE RULES IN THIS MOSAIC SCENE.

across the sandy floor, followed by slaves carrying their arms and armor. The crowd of 50,000 spectators roared with delight. When the gladiators came to a halt in front of the emperor's platform, however, the cheering stopped. Raising their right hands toward the emperor, the gladiators chanted these famous Latin words, "*Ave, Imperator, morituri te salutant!*" ("Hail, Emperor, those who are about to die salute thee!").

Gladiators in action

Games held at the Colosseum followed a set pattern. The day started with animal hunts, held in the morning. The mood changed at midday when criminals were executed. This was a foretaste for the highlight of the day – the gladiatorial contests held in the afternoon. At a large event there could be hundreds of gladiators in action. Smaller shows made do with fewer fighters, a typical number being about 30.

Dressed in purple cloaks embroidered in gold, the fighters walked through the Colosseum's gladiatorial entrances. Once inside the great building they marched

Know your enemy

In full view of the crowd, so that no one could be accused of cheating, the gladiators found out who they were to fight. The holder of the games and the gladiators' teachers decided how the men were to be paired, one against one. They usually matched men of equal fighting ability against each other. A fighter who had survived five fights might be paired against an opponent of the same rank. Mass fights between whole troops of gladiators were held only at the largest games.

The contest began with warmup fights. No one got badly hurt, since only blunt wooden weapons were used. Their purpose was to get the gladiators in the fighting spirit, and to excite the crowd.

There were at least 16 (maybe as many as 20) different types of gladiator. Men were trained to fight as one particular type, ranging from a lightly armed *secutor* ("chaser") or *retiarius* ("net-fighter") to a more heavily armed *thrax* ("Thracian") and *myrmillo* ("fish-man," named after the fish emblem on his helmet). Each one was instantly recognizable by the crowd, and spectators knew how each type of gladiator would fight.

At a sign from the holder of the games, the band began to play. Musicians sounded

LOG ON...
www.murphsplace.com/
gladiator/glads.html

MAXIMUS (RIGHT), THE HERO OF THE BLOCKBUSTER MOVIE *GLADIATOR*, FIGHTS FOR HIS LIFE IN THE ARENA.

THE SHRILL SOUND OF TRUMPETS ADDED DRAMA TO THE CONTEST.

trumpets, flutes, horns, and wheezy water organs, and amid this noise the fighting began.

Who fought whom

Several pairs of gladiators fought at the same time, with certain types often matched against each other. For example, a *myrmillo* usually fought a *thrax*. The *myrmillo* was armed with a short sword called a *gladius* (from which we get the word "gladiator"). He carried a tall, rectangular wooden shield, and was protected by head, arm, and leg armor. A *thrax* carried a smaller shield and fought with a short, curved sword. He too was protected by armor, but, like the *myrmillo*, his torso was bare, providing visible flesh for his opponent to strike at.

Occasionally, some pairs were of the same type, such as when two net-fighters came face to face. Each tried to snare the other with his net and then stab him with his trident.

Rules are rules

Movies often give the impression that gladiators fought like madmen, exchanging wild blows with each other. They didn't. The truth is that gladiator duels were skillful fights with strict rules to follow. Unfortunately, we don't know much about the rules. What we do know is that referees had the power to halt a fight. For instance, if a piece of armor fell off, the referees could stop the fight while the man put it back on – and then the fight continued.

Delivering the knockout blow

In case the fighters had "fixed" a contest agreeing who should win, referees sent slaves in to thrash the gladiators with leather straps, or threaten them with red-hot irons if they weren't fighting hard enough. It was all part of the entertainment, and the crowd loved it. As blood began to flow, the cheering increased. And when a gladiator fell to the floor, he knew the fatal blow could soon be on its way.

A fallen gladiator had one chance for survival. As he lay on his back, he raised his left hand to appeal for mercy. If the man had fought well, the crowd might want him to live. People waved their handkerchiefs, raised their thumbs, and called out, "*Mitte!*" ("Let him go!"). Then all eyes turned to see whether the giver of the games would agree. If he did, the man

was pardoned…but next time he might not be so lucky.

If the crowd thought the man had put on a poor performance, they showed no mercy. As their thumbs turned down and cries of "*Iugula!*" ("Kill him!") rang in his ears, the victim knew he was about to meet his end. Again, the games' sponsor had the last word. If he turned his thumb down, it was the signal

IN THE FILM SPARTACUS, THE REBEL GLADIATOR (RIGHT), ARMED AS A THRACIAN, GRAPPLES WITH A NET-FIGHTER.

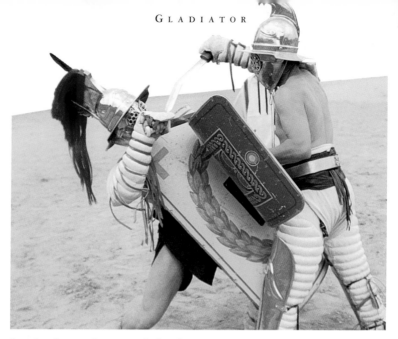

GLADIATORS USUALLY FOUGHT TO THE DEATH. MOST MEN WHO DIED IN THE ARENA WERE AGED BETWEEN 18 AND 25.

for the doomed man to "take the iron" and be finished off. His opponent executed him where he lay, and the people shouted, "*Habet!*" ("That's got him!").

Thumbs up or thumbs down? Here's a puzzle that continues to baffle historians. No one can be totally certain if "thumbs down" really was the sign of the death sentence. Some experts think we've got it dead wrong. They say "thumbs down" meant "put the sword away," as if sliding it back into its scabbard, whereas "thumbs up" meant "stick it in him." The fact is, we just don't know.

The prevailing view seems to be that the Romans used the "thumbs down" gesture when they wanted a man to die – which just shows how easy it is to believe so-called "facts" which might, in fact, turn out to be fiction!

WINNING GLADIATORS DID A LAP OF HONOR AROUND THE ARENA, WEARING LAUREL WREATHS AND WAVING PALM BRANCHES IN THE AIR.

Winners and losers

By the end of a contest, the floor of the arena was filled with bodies and drenched in blood. The sand was raked over and seems to have had a remarkable career. He fought 34 times, won 21, drew 9, and was "let go" an astonishing 4 times. But he never took the chance to

IN EIGHT GAMES, AUGUSTUS SENT 10,000 FIGHTERS INTO THE ARENA

dead gladiators were taken away on stretchers to the mortuary, where their throats were cut. Why? To make sure they really were dead, and not trying to fake their own deaths! As for the wounded, they were patched up by doctors who made sure they would live to fight again.

And the victorious winners? These men had become the new heroes of the arena. They were presented with their winnings – money and a palm branch. For excellent results, the best fighters were given a laurel wreath to wear on their heads.

The greatest prize of all was the *rudis* – a wooden sword. It was a sign that a gladiator had been given his freedom and could retire to enjoy the money and fame he had earned. One gladiator, named Flamma,

retire. This may seem odd to us, but fighting was all that many gladiators knew. Those who did retire often returned to their gladiator schools to teach the next generation of swordsmen the brutal skills they needed to stay alive in the arena.

A GLADIATOR RAISES HIS SWORD IN TRIUMPH OVER HIS SLAIN OPPONENT.

HUNTERS AND CHARIOTEERS

The people of Rome had lots of time off work. By the AD 200s, they enjoyed 200 public holidays a year! The city's authorities knew that if the people had nothing to do in their spare time, they might get bored and start rioting. As well as gladiatorial games, the state organized other entertainment to try to keep the masses happy – and it worked.

GIRAFFES WERE JUST ONE OF THE EXOTIC ANIMALS BROUGHT TO ROME.

Animals to the slaughter

Gladiators were not the only creatures to die in the arena. Games held at the Colosseum usually combined the killing of men – and sometimes women – with the mass slaughter of animals. The general rule was that animals were slaughtered in the morning, while humans were bumped off at lunchtime and in the afternoon.

The Romans had a word for shows that featured animals – *venationes*. Strictly speaking, this word means "animal hunts," but the shows weren't always as savage as it suggests. At some events, animals were paraded before the crowd simply because they were unusual species seldom seen in Rome. Imagine being there when a giraffe went on show. People were amazed that such an odd-looking animal could exist. The Roman name for a giraffe was "spotted camel" (*camelopardalis*).

Other shows were more like modern circus acts, where dangerous animals performed tricks – perhaps a lion catching a rabbit and then letting it go gored rhinoceroses, and so on. At other times, archers shot arrows at animals from the safety of metal cages – this way there was little danger of them ending up as animal food.

Massacre in the arena
The highlight of an animal show was when the animal-fighters, the *venatores*, and their assistants, the *bestiarii*, entered the arena. Just like gladiators, these men were condemned criminals, prisoners of war, and volunteers, and they received a similar kind of training. Despite their similarity to gladiators, the public regarded animal fighters as inferior beings.

unharmed, a tiger licking the hand of its trainer, or a team of panthers pulling chariots. The crowd thought it was all fun, but killing was what they were really there for – and they soon got it. Some animal shows were little more than blood-fests, with wild animals savaging each other to death. Bears fought bulls, bulls charged at elephants, elephants

AN ENRAGED BULL AND A FEROCIOUS BEAR FIGHT TO THE DEATH, TORMENTED BY A BESTIARIUS WITH A LONG HOOK.

BLOOD POURS FROM THE CHEST OF A
LEOPARD AS AN ANIMAL FIGHTER,
WEARING LITTLE PROTECTION,
IMPALES IT ON HIS SPEAR.

Wearing little more than tunics and leg-wrappings, and armed only with long spears, animal-fighters hunted a variety of animals, from harmless rabbits to man-eating lions. The *venatores* stalked them on foot, or chased them on horseback.

32 elephants, 10 elk, 10 tigers, 60 tame lions, 10 wild lions, 30 leopards, 10 hyenas, 10 camels, 20 wild donkeys (perhaps zebras), 40 wild horses, 6 hippos, and a rhinoceros. All the animals were either killed or displayed to the crowd.

TRAINED ELEPHANTS WROTE IN THE SAND WITH THEIR TRUNKS

The *bestiarii* were on standby to whip the animals into a rage, making the show even more cruel than it already was.

Some idea of the different types of animal seen in the Colosseum comes from a show organized by Emperor Philip the Arab in AD 247 to celebrate the 1,000th birthday of Rome. Records show that there were

Virtual reality hunts
But why were the Romans so cruel to animals? Well, you might think they were cruel, but most Romans didn't think like this. Hunting animals was a favorite Roman blood sport, and watching a hunt in the arena was a reminder of this. Most people who lived in Rome never left the city, so

they had little chance of going on a real hunt in the nearby fields and forests. For these city dwellers, a show in the arena was their equivalent of "virtual reality," where the countryside appeared before their eyes, complete with wild animals, scenery, trees…and hunters.

Animals were transported to Rome from all over the empire. Africa supplied lions, leopards, monkeys, crocodiles, hippos, rhinos, and ostriches. Elephants traveled from Africa and Asia, and wild boars came from the forests of northern Europe. At the Colosseum, animals were kept in rooms and cages under the floor of the arena. Elevators raised them to the surface where they appeared, as if by magic, through trapdoors.

LOG ON...
www.roman-empire.net/society/soc-games.html

T hrown to the beasts

The Romans learned many things from their friends and enemies – and not all of them were pleasant! For example, they got the idea of throwing criminals to wild beasts from the Carthaginians of North Africa, who used elephants to squash army deserters to death.

In Roman hands, this method of execution became a gory spectacle. Men and women who had committed serious crimes were tied to wooden

THOUSANDS OF WILD ANIMALS WERE CAPTURED AND TAKEN TO ROME FOR THE HUNTS. MANY CAME BY SHIP FROM AFRICA.

IN THIS MOSAIC OF AN ANIMAL SHOW, A MAN SENTENCED TO BE KILLED BY WILD ANIMALS IS WHEELED TO HIS DEATH. ANOTHER MAN IS ATTACKED TO HIS LEFT.

posts in the arena, where lions, leopards, and tigers ripped them to shreds. It was a slow, painful death. These executions took place at lunchtime, and many Romans were sickened by the sight – it was enough to turn their stomachs!

A visit to the racetrack

Another favorite Roman spectator sport was chariot racing. Just as the Colosseum was the biggest arena in the Roman world, the Circus Maximus ("Greatest Circus"), also in Rome, was the largest of all circuses, or racetracks. Measuring 1,970 ft (600 m) long and 260 ft (80 m) wide, the track formed a long, narrow rectangle with rounded ends. With room for about 200,000 spectators, the Circus Maximus was four times larger than the Colosseum and bigger than any of today's super-stadiums!

Charioteers were thought of as low-class people, just as gladiators and animal-fighters were. They, too,

A CHARIOTEER OF THE VENETI, OR BLUE TEAM, STANDS BY HIS HORSE.

54

were usually slaves, or freedmen (former slaves who had been granted their freedom). Some became rich and famous because they won many races, such as Pompeius Musclosus, who had 3,559 victories! The charioteers belonged to different racing clubs (*factiones* or factions), which were cheered on by fans, just as sports teams are today. There were only four clubs, and the charioteers wore the colors of their team. The *Albati* team wore white, the *Russati* wore red, the *Prasini* was the green team, and blue was the color of the *Veneti*.

CHARIOTS RACED AROUND A LONG PLINTH IN THE MIDDLE OF THE CIRCUS MAXIMUS.

The different colors made it easy for the crowd to figure out who was who as the chariots charged around the track.

The horses came from Spain, Greece, and North Africa, and some became as well-known as the charioteers themselves. By today's standards, Roman horses were larger than a pony, but smaller than a full-sized modern horse. Horses usually pulled chariots in teams of two or four, harnessed side by side, but sometimes up to 10 were used.

On your marks, get set, go! A race day began with a parade. It was a chance for the public to view the charioteers and bet on who they thought would win. On a signal from

the race starter, the gates of the starting boxes were flung open and the chariots thundered out. At the Circus Maximus, up to 12 chariots raced at a time, driving counterclockwise around the track for seven laps. They covered 3.2 miles (5.2 km), reaching speeds of up to 46 mph (75 kmh). Races probably lasted between 8 and 9 minutes.

WEIRD WORLD

CURSES, WRITTEN ON PIECES OF LEAD, WERE SOMETIMES BURIED AT THE RACETRACK BY PEOPLE WHO WANTED A PARTICULAR CHARIOTEER TO HAVE AN ACCIDENT, SO THAT THEIR OWN FAVORITE WOULD WIN!

Dangers of the track
Charioteers needed all their skills, not only to control their horses but also to avoid crashing into the other chariots. But pile-ups did happen, especially at each end of the track, where there was a sharp turn. And it wasn't just the charioteers and their horses who risked their lives. Boys stood at the edge of the race track throwing water to refresh the horses and drivers – careless ones ended up under the chariot wheels.

The biggest race days at the Circus Maximus usually had 24 races a day, involving about 1,000 horses. In between races, acrobats kept the noisy crowd entertained, racing at full speed as they jumped from one horse to the next. At the end of a meeting, the winners received the same kind of prizes as victorious gladiators did – palm branches and lots of money.

THE FILM BEN HUR RECREATED A CHARIOT RACE AT THE CIRCUS MAXIMUS.

EVERYDAY LIFE

Y ou've probably seen the Colosseum on TV. You may even have visited a place where Romans lived – a town, a villa, or maybe a fort. It's difficult to imagine that these broken walls were once buildings, but to the Romans they were homes and places of work. So what was it like to live in a Roman city? What did people do, what did they eat, and what clothes did they wear?

Costume customs

Clothes were usually made from wool or linen. The basic item of clothing worn by absolutely everyone – men, women, and children – was the tunic (*tunica*). This simple, loose garment hung from the shoulders to just below the knees, like a long shirt. It could be worn with or without sleeves, and was fastened at the waist by a belt. Tunics were either plain or decorated on the front and back with vertical colored stripes (*clavi*).

Men and woman also wore the same types of shoes. Leather sandals and slippers (*socci*) were worn indoors, while boots were worn outdoors. Peasants and slaves wore clogs with hard-wearing wooden soles.

WOMEN WORE EARRINGS AND NECKLACES. THEIR HAIR WAS TIED BACK AND HELD IN PLACE WITH PINS AND RIBBONS.

What did Romans wear under their tunics? That's an extremely personal question! If you must know, men and women wore a loincloth (*subligaculum*). It was a loose-fitting cloth worn around the hips like a kilt. (This was the only thing that gladiators wore under their armor!) Women

MOST MEN WORE WHITE-COLORED TOGAS. DARK ONES WERE WORN DURING TIMES OF MOURNING.

wore tight linen or leather bands around their chests. They were the equivalent of corsets, but some wore them over their tunics rather than underneath.

Heavyweight garment

Over the tunic, some men wore a heavy garment called a *toga*. Its name probably comes from the Latin word *tegere*, meaning "to cover" – which is exactly what it did. Made from a single piece of fabric, usually semicircular in shape, the *toga* was large enough to cover the man from head to toe. It was so big

THESE WOMEN ARE IN THEIR OUTDOOR CLOTHES. EACH WOMAN HAS A SHAWL DRAPED OVER HER STOLA.

PALLA

STOLA

SANDALS

that a man usually needed someone to help him drape it around his body in the correct way. Like the tunic, the *toga* could be decorated with bands of color. It was mainly worn on formal occasions, particularly by officials. Workers and slaves wore simpler clothes.

S lip into a *stola*

The *stola* was the standard item of outer clothing for women. It was a long gown worn with a chest belt that caused it to hang down in folds. Some gowns had sleeves, some didn't – it was a matter of taste. Over her *stola* (especially if she was outside) a woman wore a *palla*, which was a long shawl. She might also wear a scarf, tied at her neck.

F ather of the family

In Roman society, a "family" meant much more than a mother, a father, and their children. It also included the wives of the family's sons, and their children too. For much of Roman history, fathers were the heads of their families. It was a father's duty to provide for his family and educate his children.

When a child was born into a Roman family, the father had a choice to make – whether to recognize it as his, or not. If he took the baby in his arms, it was the sign of welcome into his family. If he did not pick the child up, it showed that he wanted nothing to do with it, and the infant was left outside

---

WEIRD WORLD

THE ROMAN WRITER PLINY THE ELDER (AD 23–79) RECOMMENDED THAT SPIDERS' WEBS BE APPLIED TO CUTS FROM SHAVING TO STOP THE BLEEDING!

LOG ON...
www.crystalinks.com/
romeclothing.html

to die. Its one and only chance of survival was if a stranger found it, in which case the child would be brought up as a slave.

Child-killing seems so cruel to us. But a new baby was another mouth to feed. If the child was born to a poor family, where the father couldn't provide any more food, it's not difficult to see why he might choose to let it die.

By about AD 200, a father's right of life or death over his children had more or less come to an end. From then on, a father who committed such a terrible act was guilty of murder.

Naming baby

Boys were named nine days after they were born, and girls when they were eight days old. At a naming ceremony, prayers were said and the baby was given a lucky charm (*bulla*) to wear around its neck. A boy wore his *bulla* until his 16th birthday. Only then could he remove it to show that he had become an adult.

Women and marriage

A girl removed her *bulla* on her wedding day – usually when she was 14 or 15. That was the day she was "placed in the

hands," as the Romans said, of her husband. From then on, she was his responsibility, not her father's. Boys were allowed to marry from the age of 14, although most married in their late teens or early twenties.

Most marriages were arranged between a girl's father and her future husband. A girl might not even know the name of her husband-to-be until after her father had decided who

CHILDREN PLAYED WITH TOYS SUCH AS DOLLS, MODEL SOLDIERS AND ANIMALS, HOOPS, AND MARBLES.

and he received a dowry (a gift of money) from her father.

June was thought to be the best time to hold a wedding, since it was the month of the goddess Juno, whose duty it was to protect marriages. At the ceremony, the couple signed a contract to pledge themselves to each other, prayers were said, and sacrifices were offered to the gods. After enjoying a feast of food and wine, the couple went to live in the groom's house.

Married women were respected members of

she was going to marry! An engagement party was held at which the girl was given a betrothal ring by her fiancé,

Roman society. They could come and go from their homes as they wished, give orders to the family's slaves (if they had any), and they could join their husbands at banquets. Despite this, women were still expected to do the shopping, look after the home, and raise children.

Home sweet home

Roman townhouses were of two types — private ones for the wealthy, and apartments for the poor. However, if you were very rich, you might have owned a big house in the countryside. This was your villa — a place to escape to on weekends, far from the noise and dirt of the town.

A townhouse (*domus*) was a single-story building lived in by a family and its servants. Unlike a modern house, the *domus* had no windows on the outside. Roman houses were designed to look in on themselves, not out. They were built around two open spaces — a hallway (*atrium*) and a garden (*peristylium*). The bedrooms, kitchen, dining rooms, servants' quarters, and storerooms were all arranged around the hallway and garden. Rooms were warmed by a heating system that circulated warm air under the floors and behind the walls. The house was very private, with no danger of being overlooked by nosy neighbors.

POOR PEOPLE LIVED IN THE UPPER STORIES OF APARTMENT BLOCKS, ABOVE OPEN-FRONTED SHOPS ON THE GROUND FLOOR.

If you weren't so wealthy and lived in an apartment block, you would have gotten to know your neighbors very well. Never mind about waving at them from your window, you could have leaned out and touched them! Rome's apartment blocks, up to five stories tall, housed the city's poor in cramped conditions. The rooms were small and dark, cold and dirty. There was no running water, no heating, and no toilets – guess what went out of the window! To brighten up their squalid surroundings, some people grew flowers in window boxes.

A BANQUET WITH MANY COURSES TOOK SEVERAL HOURS TO EAT. PEOPLE ATE WITH THEIR FINGERS, OR WITH KNIVES AND SPOONS – THE ROMANS DIDN'T USE FORKS.

What's on the menu?

At dawn, after a good night's sleep in your comfortable townhouse, or a restless one if your noisy neighbors had kept

you awake in your apartment, it was time to rise and shine and get dressed. Before the day's work began, there was just enough time to grab a cup of water and a mouthful of food for the first meal of the day, usually something cold from the previous night. The midday meal was much the same – more of yesterday's leftovers, or a piece of bread and some fruit. It was really just a snack.

The main meal of the day was dinner (*cena*). For the rich, this was a feast that might start at three in the afternoon and go on to late at night. It was eaten, after the daily bath, in the dining room (*triclinium*). On three sides of the room were low couches where the family and their guests reclined, lying on their left sides. In the middle was a table, on which the food was placed – and lots of it. Some banquets had separate courses of fish, snails, meat, vegetables, birds, fruit, nuts, and pastries.

Time for a bath

People didn't bother to wash when they woke up, since they knew they'd be having a bath later in the day – and what a bath it was! Only the best of houses had bathrooms, so

65

THE ROMAN BATHS AT THE TOWN OF AQUAE SULIS (BATH) IN ENGLAND.

most people cleaned up at the public baths (*thermae*). Town baths were usually large buildings – the baths built in Rome by Emperor Caracalla had room for 1,600 visitors at a time!

Men and women bathed at different times – mixed bathing was not allowed. After undressing, bathers went through to a very hot room (*sudatorium*), where they sweated for a while. It was like a modern sauna. Then they went to a not-so-hot room (*caldarium*), where they rubbed their bodies with oil. When they scraped off the oil, the day's grime came off with it. After that came a dip in a lukewarm pool (in the *tepidarium*), a plunge into a cold pool (in the *frigidarium*), and, last of all, a massage with scented oils in the *unctuarium*.

Taking a bath was a social occasion too – a chance to talk, gossip, and catch up on the news.

Water supply

Roman cities needed vast amounts of water for bathing, drinking, and washing waste away from their lavatories. Much of this was supplied by aqueducts. These were waterways that channeled water from rivers, lakes, and springs to builtup

THE CONTAINER ABOVE HELD OIL, WHICH WAS SPRINKLED ON A PERSON'S SKIN. A METAL SCRAPER CALLED A STRIGIL (ABOVE LEFT) WAS USED TO REMOVE IT.

66

areas, using tunnels and huge stone bridges to overcome hills, valleys, and any other obstacles that stood in their way.

Relatives, flute players, and professional mourners (whose job was to wail and cry) walked slowly in a funeral procession

IT WAS POLITE TO BURP, SPIT, AND PASS GAS AT MEALTIMES!

Health, death, and burial
Romans suffered from the same diseases and illnesses as we do, but their life expectancy was shorter. Only the wealthy, who ate good food and could afford doctors and medical treatment, lived past their 60th birthday. The poor were lucky to reach their 40s or 50s. Rich people were usually cremated after they died, while the poor were buried.

toward a cemetery outside the town. At a rich person's funeral, relatives wore masks to represent the dead person's ancestors – it was a way of bringing the family together. But whatever their background, all Romans hoped to go to Elysium – the Roman version of heaven.

THE PONT DU GARD, SOUTHERN FRANCE, WAS BOTH AN AQUEDUCT (TOP LEVEL) AND A ROAD BRIDGE (BOTTOM LEVEL).

THE ARTS OF ROME

E very civilization has its artistic side,
and the Romans certainly had theirs.
There was so much more to Roman life than
trips to the savage arena and the thrills and
spills racetrack. Romans prided themselves on being
educated, artistic, and cultured people. To them, it was
everyone else who was brutal and barbaric.

Getting an education

There were no laws that said
children had to go to school, and
many, especially the children of
poor people, had no schooling
at all. Education was entirely
the responsibility of your
parents. So, if
you grew up not
knowing how
to read, write,
or count, you
could blame it
on them!

Children from
the rich part of
town tended to
be privately
educated at home
by their own
personal teachers,
who were usually
slaves or freedmen.

Most other children were
packed off to schools around
town. Schools consisted of a
room rented by a teacher at the
back of a shop, with just a
curtain to separate the shoppers
from the scholars.

A TEACHER GIVES A
LESSON TO A GROUP
OF PUPILS

PART OF A
WOODEN
WRITING
TABLET

BRONZE
INK PEN

POINTED
STYLUS

INK POT

MOST WRITING WAS DONE IN INK ON
THIN SHEETS OF WOOD OR PAPYRUS, OR
SCRATCHED ONTO A WAX TABLET WITH A
WRITING TOOL CALLED A STYLUS.

School days

Boys and girls usually began school at the age of seven. In Rome, the school day started early, usually just after dawn. Sitting on wooden stools and facing the teacher perched on his high chair, elementory school children learned to read and write. Their teacher was known as a *litterator* – "one who teaches letters." Another teacher, called the *calculator*, taught them simple math. Children learned by copying and reciting letters, sentences, and numbers over and over again.

At age 10 or 11, some boys went to grammar school. Girls stopped going to school and stayed at home until they got married. The grammar school

THE ROMAN WOMAN IN THIS PAINTING HOLDS A STYLUS AND A WAX TABLET. THE MAN CLASPS A BOOK ROLL.

From the age of 14 or 15, a few boys were taught by a *rhetor*. He had a real schoolroom, paid for by the state, where he taught the art of oratory. Pupils learned how to speak fluently, ordering their thoughts clearly and choosing their words carefully. By the age of 20, these young men were ready to start their working lives. Those that had mastered oratory often worked in the law or in politics, where public speaking was important.

teacher was a *grammaticus*. Boys attended this school, also behind a shop, for up to five years. They learned the rules (grammar) that governed the Latin language, read books by famous authors, and learned Greek – the Roman Empire's second language.

Books and libraries

A good education meant you'd be able to read books and poems by Roman and Greek writers. But they weren't books like this one, with pages

THE LIBRARY OF CELSUS AT THE ROMAN CITY OF EPHESUS, TURKEY, ONCE HELD 12,000 BOOKS.

A ROMAN THEATER RESEMBLED AN ARENA WITH THE END CHOPPED OFF.

you can turn. Roman books were written by hand (the Romans didn't know about printing) on sheets of paper made from the Egyptian papyrus plant. Black and red ink was used. Mistakes could be rubbed out with a damp sponge. The finished sheets were glued together into rolls, each of about 100 sheets, then wrapped around a winding stick (*umbilicus*). These "book rolls" were stored on their sides in the bookcases of a library (*bibliotheca*). Finally, labels were attached to the book rolls to give their titles.

Watching a play

A visit to the theater was a popular pastime in towns and cities throughout the empire. Roman theaters didn't put on performances whenever they felt like it, as theaters do today. Instead, a theater only opened its doors to the public when other shows were on in town, such as a gladiatorial contest at the local arena, or a chariot race down at the track. The Roman officials were eager to offer the people a wide range of events to choose from when the games came to town. It was your choice – blood and guts at the arena, or laughs and hisses at the theater!

71

At first sight, a theater, such as Rome's 12,000-seat Theater of Marcellus, looks like half an arena. But the way you should really see it is the other way around – an arena is like two theaters joined together to make a circular (or oval) building. This is why an arena is known as an amphitheater, which means "double-theater."

Playing for laughs

Plays were performed in the afternoons, at the same time that gladiators were hacking lumps off each other in the arena. While theatergoers were booing a bad actor, or pelting him with apples (never tomatoes, which didn't exist in Europe until the 1500s), people at the games might be sentencing a gladiator to death! However, Roman theaters enjoyed their share of sidesplitting, too – laughter that is. People loved to see a rib-tickling comedy. Audiences showed their appreciation for well-performed plays by snapping their fingers, clapping, and, if it was really good, waving handkerchiefs and corners of their clothes. Serious plays, called tragedies, were just as popular, but without the laughs (maybe a few tears).

ACTORS WORE MASKS THAT LET THE AUDIENCE KNOW WHETHER THE PLAY WAS A TRAGEDY OR A COMEDY. THIS MASK WAS WORN IN A COMEDY.

Pictures in paint

The Romans were expert craft-workers. They excelled in decorating the walls, floors, and ceilings of their public and

A WALL PAINTING OF A RIOT IN AD 59 AT POMPEII'S ARENA. THE SHADE, OR CANOPY, IS AT THE TOP OF THE PICTURE.

private buildings with pictures. Paintings were often designed to suit the function of the room in which they appeared. For example, pictures of fish and river scenes appeared in the baths; and the dining rooms of houses featured hunting images, dead animals, and banquets.

Artists painted rooms with panels and bands of bright color, particularly red. Some walls were decorated with landscape scenes, flowers, or figures from Greek and Roman mythology. To our eyes, these bright colored rooms can seem overdone, but to the Romans they were the height of fashion and good taste.

We're lucky that any of these fragile paintings have survived at all, but many have. Some are documentary images, recording scenes from real life, just as newspaper photographs do today. An instance of this can be seen in a wall painting from Pompeii, a small town south of Rome, where an unknown artist painted a riot scene. The riot happened in AD 59, in and around the town's arena. The painting not only shows us the

fight between the Pompeiians and visitors from Nuceria, but it also shows the arena's seats, stairways, entrances, and canopy.

Craft of the mosaic maker

If there's one Roman craft that everyone's heard of, it's mosaic. But did you know that mosaic – the art of making pictures from small cubes of colored stone, glass, or pottery – was actually invented by the Greeks, not the Romans? It's another example of how the Romans copied other people's good ideas. However, in the hands of the Roman mosaicists (that's the name for people who make mosaics), the craft reached perfection. The mosaics were made by laying different-colored stone cubes, some just 0.2 in (5 mm) across, in wet plaster.

Mosaics were mainly used on floors, but some walls were also decorated with mosaic pictures. Like paintings, there was a range of mosaic styles to suit a person's taste and budget. The cheapest mosaics were simple

Glassware and pottery

The Romans were also skilled glassworkers. Flasks and bottles were mass-produced by blowing glass into molds. Fine glassware might have bands of gold running through it.

Potters were kept busy making

ONE HOUSE IN POMPEII HAD A "BEWARE OF THE DOG" MOSAIC

geometric patterns – squares, triangles, or diamonds – often made from large, roughly shaped cubes, or even pebbles. These patterns could be repeated over and over again until the whole floor was covered. More costly mosaics used tiny cubes to make highly detailed, lifelike images of people, gods, and animals. Cubes of pure gold, rock-crystal, and rare marble were used in the most luxurious mosaics, giving them a stunning, jewel-like quality.

all kinds of ceramic vessels, from clay lamps, bowls, and cups to large storage vessels (amphorae) used to hold wine and oil. Pottery was often decorated with molded pictures or, sometimes, given a glaze, which gave its surface a shiny, glasslike look. Many of the images on pots and in mosaics and paintings were of gods, goddesses, and scenes from the Roman religion, which was at the heart of Roman life.

THIS BEAUTIFUL ROMAN VASE WAS MADE FROM BLUE AND WHITE GLASS.

GODS AND TEMPLES

For most of their long history, the Romans believed in many gods and goddesses. These powerful beings were thought to watch over and control every aspect of daily life. As long as people kept faith in the gods, then good things would happen. To make sure of this, people offered gifts to the gods in their homes and at temples.

Houses for the gods

Roman temples were houses for the gods to live in. Don't think of them as being like churches, synagogues, or mosques – because they weren't. While people today worship inside religious buildings, the Romans performed their acts of devotion outside the temples, at altars nearby. The inside of a Roman temple was dark and virtually empty, except for the statue of the god whose temple it was. People believed that the god's spirit lived inside the statue.

Gifts great and small

People sought favors from the gods. In repayment, they offered

BEFORE THE SACRIFICE OF A BULL, A PRIEST IS SHOWN PURIFYING THE AIR BY BURNING SWEET-SMELLING INCENSE ON A FIRE.

gifts, usually anything they could afford, from a few hairs plucked from the head to an animal such as a pig, a sheep, or a chicken. The bigger the animal, the greater the gift – and gifts didn't come much bigger or more expensive than an ox.

There were rules to follow when animals were slaughtered. Male animals were sacrificed to male gods, and female animals to goddesses. Some gods preferred certain animals, some religious festivals demanded pigs not sheep, and so on.

After the animal had been knocked unconscious, its throat was cut – except if it was a chicken, in which case its neck was wrung. The dead animal was disemboweled and its guts were examined by priests (what a job!) in search of omens. A healthy liver was a good sign, but a diseased liver meant that someone was in for bad luck.

JUPITER, KNOWN BY THE GREEKS AS ZEUS, WAS THE KING OF THE ROMAN GODS. SOME EMPERORS BELIEVED THAT THEY WERE JUPITER HIMSELF, COME TO LIVE ON EARTH.

Household shrines

You didn't have to take a trip to the local temple to offer a gift to the gods. Every Roman family – whether rich or poor – had an altar, or *lararium*, at home. The father, as head of the household, made offerings on behalf of his family. Each morning he said prayers to the household spirits (*lares*) and left bread, fruit, and maybe some wine on the altar.

Happy families

The Romans had a family of 12 main gods and goddesses. What a coincidence, so did the Greeks! How come? Well, the Romans adopted the Greeks' gods, gave them Roman names, and then worshipped them as their own. So Zeus, the chief god of the Greeks, became the Roman god

THE MEANING OF THIS MOSAIC IS THAT AS TIME ROLLS ON (THE WHEEL), DEATH WILL INEVITABLY COME (THE SKULL).

Jupiter. Hera, his wife, became the Roman goddess Juno; Athena became Minerva; Ares became Mars, and so on.

But it wasn't just Greek gods that the Romans adopted. Isis, an Egyptian goddess, and Mithras, a Persian deity, were also worshipped by some Romans. Instead of stamping out the foreign religions they encountered when they took over new lands, the Romans often incorporated the local beliefs into their own religion. The Romans tolerated people of all religions except those, like Christians, who refused to worship the emperor as well.

Death and beyond

The Romans believed in life after death. To them, heaven was a place of eternal peace and happiness – but first they had to get there. The dead were buried Asphodel (the place for good citizens). If the judges decided a soul had lived a bad life and offended the gods, it was sent to Tartarus, the Roman version of hell. After a very, very long time

EACH FAMILY HAD ITS OWN GUARDIAN SPIRIT, OR GENIUS

with a small coin under their tongue. This was to pay Charon, the ferryman who rowed souls across the Styx River – the great river that flowed around the Underworld (land of the dead).

Once across the Styx, souls passed Cerberus – a monstrous, three-headed guard dog who prevented souls from sneaking back over the Styx to the land of the living.

Three judges asked souls to account for their life on Earth. The souls then drank water from the Lethe River, which made them forget their past lives.

Most souls were sent to Elysium (the place for warriors or heroes) or to the Plain of

in Tartarus, the soul might be allowed to travel to Elysium.

Religion of the Christians

In the 1st century AD, in the Roman province of Judea (modern-day Israel, Palestine, and Jordan), a new religion began. It quickly gained many converts, who became known as

TWO SOULS STEP INTO CHARON'S BOAT TO BE ROWED OVER THE STYX RIVER.

CRUCIFIXION WAS A CRUEL, SHAMEFUL DEATH. THIS SMALL IVORY CARVING, MADE BY CHRISTIANS IN THE AD 400S, DEPICTS THE CRUCIFIXION OF JESUS.

Christians. They were followers of the teachings of Jesus of Nazareth. Some Jewish people believed that Jesus was the Son of God – the Messiah, or Christ, who would free them from their Roman oppressors. Other Jews disagreed and demanded, in AD 33, that the Romans execute him. Fearing disorder, the Romans had Jesus crucified – nailed to a wooden cross and left there to die. The Romans hoped

that Jesus's death would settle the matter. But his followers stayed together, and within a few years a faith had grown up around his memory.

Treated like criminals

By the AD 50s, the new religion (Christianity) had reached Rome. Christians were seen as a threat, because their belief in one supreme god challenged the Roman belief in many gods. Rome persecuted Christians who would not worship other gods. Christians were forced to

WEIRD WORLD
DID CHRISTIANS DIE IN THE COLOSSEUM? MAYBE, MAYBE NOT. CONTRARY TO POPULAR BELIEF, THERE IS NO EVIDENCE THAT CHRISTIANS WERE EVER KILLED THERE.

hold their meetings in secret. Rumors spread that they were involved in criminal activities.

When a large part of Rome was destroyed by fire in AD 64, Emperor Nero blamed the Christians for starting it. From then on, a new spectacle was seen in the city. Nero rounded up Christians and had them executed – some were tied to posts, covered in pitch, and set on fire. These human torches burned through the night in the grounds of Nero's palace. He treated others like common criminals and had them either beheaded or thrown to the beasts in the city's arena (a wooden one that existed until the Colosseum was built some years later).

However, this persecution had little effect in curbing the spread of the Christian religion. In time, it proved stronger even than the might of Rome itself.

IN THIS IMAGINATIVE PAINTING, MADE IN THE 1800S, CHRISTIANS ARE KILLED BY WILD ANIMALS IN A ROMAN ARENA.

DECLINE AND FALL

Nothing lasts forever. Not the cruel Colosseum, not the gory games, not even the mighty Roman Empire. By the AD 300s, Rome was struggling to keep out the barbarian tribes that were attacking the frontiers of its territory. To make things worse, emperors and would-be emperors were constantly fighting among themselves. And as for the Christians…well, they just wouldn't go away.

Historic moment

The Battle of the Milvian Bridge, fought outside the city of Rome in October, AD 312, was a turning point in Roman history. At this battle, Constantine, an army general, defeated his rival Maxentius and became emperor. Before the battle, Constantine had a vision in which the Christian god showed a cross to him and said, "In this sign, conquer!" He believed that the god of the Christians had come to his aid. In gratitude, Constantine allowed Christians to worship as they wished. The days of persecution were over, and the first Christian churches were built in Rome.

EMPEROR CONSTANTINE STOPPED THE PERSECUTION OF CHRISTIANS. HE STARTED TO FOLLOW CHRISTIAN WAYS HIMSELF.

Goodbye gladiators

As more and more Romans began to reject their gods for the Christian faith, people also grew unhappy with the brutal games and animal fights still being staged at the Colosseum.

In AD 326, Constantine decided to abolish gladiatorial games – but that wasn't the end of the fighting men altogether. Some emperors that came after him, such as the pagan (non-Christian) emperor Julian, tried to revive the bloody spectacles. However, the "golden age" of gladiators had come to an end.

By AD 391, under Emperor Theodosius, all forms of pagan (pre-Christian) sacrifice had been banned and temples to the old gods closed. Then, in AD 399, the gladiatorial schools were shut down by Emperor Honorius. The final nail in the gladiators' coffin came in about AD 400. The story goes that Almachius, a Christian monk, ran into the Colosseum's arena and tried to separate two gladiators. He was killed either by the angry crowd or by the gladiators on the orders of the Roman officials. Honorius was so disgusted by this that he banned gladiator shows forever, although animal hunts carried on for another 200 years.

LOG ON...
www.roman-empire.net/children/achieve.html

THE ABANDONED COLOSSEUM BECAME A RUIN. ITS STONES WERE CARTED AWAY TO MAKE NEW BUILDINGS ELSEWHERE IN ROME.

B eginning of the end

By the late AD 300s, barbarian tribes, such as the Visigoths and Vandals, were moving into Roman territory. Legions were recalled from the farthest outposts of the empire to defend Rome, but they couldn't stop the Visigoths from destroying much of the city in AD 410. The empire was falling apart.

A New Rome

In AD 476, Romulus Augustulus saved himself from the swords of the barbarians by letting them have the fabulous city of Rome – and with it the rest of the Roman Empire in western Europe. This 16-year-old boy entered the history books as the last true emperor of Rome.

Roman ways continued for several hundred years in the eastern part of the empire, where a "New Rome" had been built, named Constantinople (now Istanbul, in modern Turkey). But one thing had gone forever – gladiators.

ALARIC, KING OF THE VISIGOTHS, ENTERS ROME WITH HIS WARRIORS IN AD 410.

REFERENCE SECTION

Whether you've finished reading *Gladiator*, or are turning to this section first, you'll find the information on the next eight pages really helpful. Here are all the historical facts, figures, dates, background details, and unfamiliar words that you will need. You'll also find a list of website addresses – so, whether you want to surf the net or search out facts, these pages should turn you from an enthusiast into an expert.

THE EMPERORS OF ROME

This list names many (but not all) of the men who called themselves emperors of Rome, and the dates of their reigns. At certain times in Rome's history, two or more men claimed the title of emperor at the same time. There were rare times when there was no clear emperor at all. After the empire split in AD 284, there were usually separate emperors for the Eastern and Western empires.

Julio-Claudian dynasty

27 BC–AD 14	Augustus
14–37	Tiberius
37–41	Caligula
41–54	Claudius
54–68	Nero

Civil war of AD 69

68–69	Galba
69	Vitellius
69	Otho

Flavian dynasty

69–79	Vespasian
79–81	Titus
81–96	Domitian

Adoptive emperors

96–98	Nerva
98–117	Trajan
117–138	Hadrian
138–161	Antoninus Pius
161–180	Marcus Aurelius
161–169	Lucius Verus
180–192	Commodus

Civil war of AD 193

193	Pertinax
193	Didius Julianus
193–194	Pescennius Niger
193–194	Clodius Albinus

Severan dynasty

193–211	Septimius Severus
211–217	Caracalla
211	Geta

217–218	Macrinus
218	Diadumenianus
218–222	Elagabalus
222–235	Severus Alexander

Time of chaos

235–238	Maximinus Thrax
238	Gordian I
238	Gordian II
238	Pupienus / Balbinus
238–244	Gordian III
244–249	Philip the Arab
249–251	Decius
251–253	Trebonianus Gallus
253	Aemilius Aemilianus
253–260	Valerian
253–268	Gallienus

Gallic emperors

260–269	Postumus
269	Laelianus
269	Marius
268–271	Victorinus
271–274	Tetricus

Illyrian emperors

268–270	Claudius II
270	Quintillus
270–275	Aurelian
275–276	Tacitus
276	Florianus
276–282	Probus
282–283	Carus
283–284	Numerian
283–285	Carinus
284–285	Julian I

Empire restored

284–305	Diocletian
286–308	Maximian
305–306	Constantius I
305–311	Galerius
306–307	Severus II
306–312	Maxentius
310–313	Maximius Daia
308–324	Licinius

House of Constantine

306–337	Constantine I
337–340	Constantine II
337–350	Constans
337–361	Constantius II
360–363	Julian II
364–365	Jovian

House of Valentinian

364–375	Valentinian I (West)
364–378	Valens (East)
367–383	Gratian (West)
375–392	Valentinian II (West)

House of Theodosius

379–395	Theodosius I
393–408	Arcadius (East)
395–423	Honorius (West)
402–450	Theodosius II (East)

423–425	Johannes (West)
425–455	Valentinian III (West)

Other claimants to the title

During this time, many other men tried to become emperor, sometimes ruling whole regions until they were toppled. Here are a few of them.

286–293	Carausius
350–353	Magnentius
360–366	Procopius
380–388	Magnus Maximus
392–394	Eugenius
407–411	Constantine III
409–411	Maximus
411–413	Jovinus

Last Western emperors

455	Petronius Maximus
455–456	Avitus
457–461	Majorian
461–465	Severus III
466	*(no emperor)*
467–472	Anthemius
472	Olybrius
473–474	Glycerius
474–480	Julius Nepos
475–476	Romulus Augustulus

GLADIATOR WHO'S WHO

Andabata ("blind-fighter")
Wore chain mail and a fully visored helmet, closed so he could not see out. He found his enemy, usually another *andabata*, by groping blindly around, then thrust a sword at him.

Cruppellarius ("mail-clad fighter")
Little is known about him. He was heavily armed and wore armor.

Dimachaerus ("two-sword fighter")
Fought with two swords or daggers.

Eques ("horseman")
Fought on horseback with a 6-ft (2-m) lance and a sword. He carried a round shield, and wore a tunic and helmet. His lower legs and sword arm were guarded by wrappings.

Essedarius ("war-chariot fighter")
Fought from a lightweight, two-wheeled war chariot. One *essedarius* fought another *essedarius*. Their style of fighting is unclear. They may not have fought from their chariots. Instead, they may have dismounted, then fought on foot.

Hoplomachus ("shield-fighter")
Was one of the most heavily armored fighters. Lower legs were protected with greaves (metal leg-guards), while on his right arm and thighs he wore padded fabric wrappings. His head and face were protected by a helmet. He carried a tiny round shield, and fought with a lance and a dagger or a short sword.

Laquerarius ("noose-fighter")
Little is known about him, except that he fought with a lasso and wore very little armor.

Myrmillo ("fish-man")
His helmet, which came down over his face, had a distinctive fishcrest. He carried a sword and a large shield. His chest was bare, but his sword arm and legs were protected with fabric wrappings. His usual opponent was a *thrax* or a *hoplomachus*.

Paegniarius ("comic-fighter")
His job was to entertain the audience with mock fights during intervals. *Paegniarius* fought with a whip, club, and a shield.

Provocator ("challenger")
Wore a greave on his left leg (his right leg was not protected). On his chest was a metal breastplate, and he wore a helmet with a visor, and an arm-guard on his sword arm. His shield was large and rectangular. *Provocator* fought with a short, straight-edged sword.

Retiarius ("net-fighter")
A lightly armed, fast-moving fighter who did not wear a helmet. Fought with a net, a three-pronged trident, and a long dagger. His left arm and shoulder were protected by guards. Apart from a loincloth, he was naked. He used his net to catch his opponent, who was usually a *secutor*. His net was weighted with small pieces of lead, which made it spread out easier and quicker when he threw it at his opponent.

Sagittarius ("archer")
Fought with a powerful bow, which fired arrows over distances of up to 660 ft (200 m).

Scissor ("carver")
Apart from his name, nothing is known about his arms or armor.

Secutor ("chaser")
Carried a large rectangular shield and wore a visored helmet. A greave protected his left leg, and padding covered his right arm. His weapon was a dagger or a short sword.

Tertiarius ("substitute fighter")
Sometimes three men were matched against each other. The first two would fight, only for the winner to be met by the third man – the *tertiarius*. Also known as a *suppositicius*.

Thrax ("Thracian")
Heavily armored. Wore a helmet with a high crest, and greaves over thin trousers. His thighs and sword arm were wrapped in fabric for protection. Carried a small, square shield. Fought with a very short, curved thrusting sword.

Velitis ("skirmisher")
Fought with a spear attached to a leash, so that after he had thrown his spear he could pull it back.

NUMBERS

Roman numerals were made up of a mixture of seven different letters:

I (1) **V** (5) **X** (10) **L** (50)
C (100) **D** (500) **M** (1,000).

They followed a logical pattern, based on addition and subtraction. For example, the number 4 was written as **IV** (1 less than 5), and 6 was **VI** (5 plus 1). The number of this page (89) written in Roman numerals is:

LXXXIX (50 + 10 + 10 + 10 + 9).

Bigger numbers didn't always mean more letters were needed. The number 99 was **IC** (1 less than 100), while 1001 was **MI** (1,000 plus 1).

1 **I**	11 **XI**	30 **XXX**
2 **II**	12 **XII**	40 **XL**
3 **III**	13 **XIII**	50 **L**
4 **IV**	14 **XIV**	60 **LX**
5 **V**	15 **XV**	100 **C**
6 **VI**	16 **XVI**	200 **CC**
7 **VII**	17 **XVII**	300 **CCC**
8 **VIII**	18 **XVIII**	400 **CD**
9 **IX**	19 **XIX**	500 **D**
10 **X**	20 **XX**	1,000 **M**

ANCIENT ROME WEBSITES

www.roman-empire.net/index.html
Huge site that calls itself the "leading web-resource on Rome." Organized into many sections on themes of interest, including a children's section.
www.geocities.com/Athens/Forum/6946/rome.html
Take a virtual tour of the city of Rome.
http://members.tripod.com/~S_van_Dorst/legio.html
The Roman army during the time of the empire.
www-2.cs.cmu.edu/~mjw/recipes/ethnic/historical/ant-rom-coll.html
Cook up an authentic Roman meal from recipes on this site.
www.bluffton.edu/~sullivanm/romancolosseum/romancolosseum.html
Colosseum photos and facts.
www.thebritishmuseum.ac.uk/world/rome/rome.html
Roman Britain and the empire. Search for items in the British Museum collection, and see photos of the objects.
www.geocities.com/Athens/Atrium/7339/
Death, burial, and funeral customs in the Roman world.
www.pantheon.org/mythica/areas/roman/
Encyclopedia Mythica has information on Roman gods and goddesses.
www.capitolium.org/english.htm
Digging and research at the website of the Roman Imperial Forums.

GODS AND GODDESSES

This list names the major Roman gods and goddesses, and also some of the many minor ones. The 12 major deities are indicated by an asterisk (*).

Apollo *
God of prophecy and healing
Greek name – Apollo

Aesculapius
God of healing
Greek name – Asclepius

Bacchus
God of wine
Greek name – Dionysos

Ceres *
Goddess of agriculture
Greek name – Demeter

Cupid
God of love
Greek name – Eros

Diana *
Goddess of the moon and hunting
Greek name – Artemis

Dis (also called Pluto)
God of the Underworld
Greek name – Hades

Faunus
God of fertility
Greek name – Pan

Hercules
God of victory and business
Greek name – Herakles

Janus
God of doorways
An entirely Roman god

Juno *
Goddess of women and marriage,
queen of the gods, wife of Jupiter
Greek name – Hera

Jupiter *
God of the heavens and weather,
king of the gods, husband of Juno
Greek name – Zeus

Mars *
God of war
Greek name – Ares

Mercury *
God of communications and
travelers
Greek name – Hermes

Minerva *
Goddess of wisdom
Greek name – Athena

Mithras
God of the sun, bringer of light
A Persian god

Neptune *
God of the oceans and earthquakes
Greek name – Poseidon

Proserpine
Goddess of the Underworld
Greek name – Persephone

Roma
Goddess of the city of Rome, who
represented the greatness of the
Roman Republic and Empire

Saturn
God of time
Greek name – Cronos

Uranus
God of the sky
Greek name – Ouranos

Venus *
Goddess of love
Greek name – Aphrodite

Vesta *
Goddess of the home and hearth
Greek name – Hestia

Vulcan *
God of fire and blacksmiths
Greek name – Hephaestus

ANCIENT ROME TIMELINE

c.1000 BC
First villages on the hills of Rome.

753 BC
Legendary founding of Rome.

c.753–509 BC
Rome ruled by kings.

509 BC
Last king overthrown, Roman Republic began.

390 BC
Rome ransacked by Gauls.

264 BC
First gladiatorial contest in Rome.

264–146 BC
Wars against Carthage, North Africa.

214–146 BC
Wars against Greece.

73–71 BC
Spartacus, a slave who became a gladiator, led a rebellion of 90,000 fellow slaves against the Romans.

59–51 BC
Gaul conquered.

45 BC
Caesar became dictator of Rome.

44 BC
Caesar assassinated – it was thought he had too much power.

27 BC
Roman Republic ended. Octavian became the first Roman emperor (Augustus). Roman Empire began.

AD 43
Conquest of Britain began.

AD 60
Queen Boudicca led a rebellion in Britain against the Roman invaders.

AD 64
Fire destroyed much of Rome. Nero began the persecution of Christians.

AD 68–69
After Nero's death, power struggles led to civil war.

AD 79
Destruction of Roman towns by the eruption of the volcano Vesuvius.

AD 80
Colosseum opened in Rome.

c.AD 120
Roman Empire at its greatest extent.

AD 120–28
Hadrian's Wall built in Britain.

AD 271
Wall built around Rome.

AD 284
Roman Empire split into Eastern and Western parts.

AD 313
Edict of Milan – Christianity and all other religions were tolerated throughout the Roman Empire.

AD 326
Constantine abolished gladiatorial contests. (They were later revived by other emperors.)

AD 330
Constantinople (Istanbul) became the "New Rome" in the east – the capital of the Roman world.

c.AD 400
Last known gladiatorial contest at the Colosseum.

AD 410
Rome ransacked by Goths.

AD 476
Abdication of Romulus Augustulus, last emperor of the Western Empire.

AD 476–1453
Eastern Empire flourished for 1,000 years, until Constantinople was conquered by the Turks.

GLOSSARY

Amphitheater
An open-air building for shows.

Amphora
A storage pot for wine or oil.

Aqueduct
A bridge for carrying water.

Arena
The floor area of an amphitheater.
Arena means "sand" in Latin.

Atrium
The entrance area of a Roman house.

Auxiliary
A soldier from a Roman province.

Ballista
A stone-throwing catapult.

Barbarian
According to the Romans, any person from outside the Roman world.

Basilica
A large public building housing law courts, offices, and shops.

Bestiarius
A performer who tormented animals in the arena.

Bulla
A lucky charm worn by children.

Calculator
A teacher who taught math.

Caldarium
The warm room at the baths.

Centurion
The commander of a century.

Century
A company of 80–100 soldiers.

Circus
A racetrack.

Citizen
Originally a man born in Rome to Roman parents. Eventually, people across the empire were granted the right to call themselves citizens.

Clavi
The stripes on Roman clothes.

Cohort
A unit of 480 soldiers in a legion.

Consul
The most senior government official.

Crucifixion
A form of execution in which a person was nailed or tied to a cross or tree.

Domus
A house in a town.

Editor
A wealthy person who sponsored a gladiatorial show.

Elysium
The Roman version of heaven.

Emperor
The ruler of the Roman world.

Empire
(1) The extent of all the provinces ruled by the Romans. (2) The time when Rome was ruled by emperors.

Etruscans
People in Italy, north of Rome, who flourished before the Romans.

Forum
The square in the middle of a Roman town, which was used for markets, politics, and processions.

Frigidarium
The cold plunge-pool at the baths.

Genius
A protecting spirit.

Gladiator
A highly trained fighter, named after his main weapon, the *gladius*.

Gladius
A short sword used by a gladiator.

Graffiti
Words scratched or painted onto a wall or other surface.

Grammaticus
A teacher who taught grammar.
Greave
A metal protector for the lower leg.
Lanista
An owner-trainer of gladiators.
Lararium
A small altar in a private house.
Lares
Spirits who protected the household.
Latin
The language of the Romans.
Latium
The homeland of the Romans in Italy.
Legate
The commanding officer of a legion.
Legion
A division of 4,000 to 6,000 soldiers.
Legionnaire
A soldier belonging to a legion.
Litterator
A teacher of reading and writing.
Ludus
A school for training gladiators.
Mosaic
A picture usually made of stone cubes.
Palla
A shawl worn by women.
Papyrus
An Egyptian water-reed from which writing paper was made.
Peristylium
The garden of a Roman house.
Pilum
The javelin used by Roman soldiers.
Praetorian Guard
The emperor's personal army.
Province
A territory of the Roman Empire.
Pugio
The dagger used by Roman soldiers.
Republic
A state or country governed by officials elected by the people.

Rhetor
A teacher who taught public speaking.
Rudis
The wooden sword given to gladiators on their retirement from the arena.
Senate
The group of elected nobles who governed Rome.
Senator
An official, a member of the Senate.
Socci
Slippers worn indoors.
Stola
The main garment worn by women.
Strigil
A scraper used to clean the body.
Stylus
A writing pen.
Sudatorium
The hottest room at the baths.
Tartarus
The Roman version of hell.
Tepidarium
The lukewarm pool at the baths.
Thermae
A Roman bath-house.
Toga
The main garment worn by men.
Tribune
A middle-ranking officer in a legion.
Triclinium
The dining room of a private house.
Tunica
A shirtlike undergarment.
Unctuarium
The massage room at the baths.
Venatio
An animal show.
Venator
An animal-hunter.
Villa
A large house in the country.
Vomitoria
Entrances and exits at an arena.

INDEX

CREDITS

Dorling Kindersley would like to thank:

Marcus James for initial design concept, Dean Price for jacket design, and Chris Bernstein for the index.

Illustration by:
Russell Barnett 18bl.

Additional photography by:
Joe Cornish, Mike Dunning, Simon James, Dave King, Liz McAulay, Karl Shone, Lin White, Alan Williams.